THE COOKING OF

MATTHEW LOCRICCHIO

WITH PHOTOS BY

JACK McCONNELL

BENCHMARK BOOKS

MARSHALL CAVENDISH
NEW YORK

This book is dedicated to the reader who picks up a spoon and a bowl and makes something good to eat, and to every reader who always wanted to.

ACKNOWLEDGMENTS

Cookbooks are the result of great teamwork and the cooperation of many people, and *The Cooking of China* is certainly no exception. Many thanks must first go to the members of the Recipe Testers Club and their adult assistant chefs, whose testing, comments, and suggestions were invaluable. They are: Saun Ellis and Sonia, Nico, and Danny Drohojowski of New Milford, Connecticut; Diane Carter, Molly Hall, and Sadie Hall of Santa Cruz, California; Lydia Aultman and William Aultman of Hudson, New York; Douglas and Sophie Madach and Victoria Aucoin of River Ridge, Louisiana; Linda Sproule of Old Chatham, New York; Virginia Locricchio Zerang and Nikolas Zerang of Glenview, Illinois; and Mary Rich and Matthew Zimmerman of Riverdale, New York. A special thank-you to Dr. Archie Karfly for his inestimable support and encouragement. Also, thanks to Xiuwen Wu, Ph.D., College of Education, Michigan State University, for her help with my Chinese, and to Delores Custer for her guidance on the recipes.

Benchmark Books
Marshall Cavendish
99 White Plains Road
Tarrytown, New York 10591-9001
www.marshallcavendish.com
Text copyright © 2003 by Matthew Locricchio
Food photographs © 2003 Jack McConnell, McConnell, McNamara & Company
Art director for food photography: Matthew Locricchio
Map copyright © 2003 by Mike Reagan

Illustrations by Janet Hamlin
Illustrations copyright © 2003 by Marshall Cavendish Corporation

Book design by Anahid Hamparian
Food styling by Marie Hirschfeld and Matthew Locricchio

Library of Congress Cataloging-in-Publication Data

Locricchio, Matthew.
  The cooking of China / by Matthew Locricchio.
      p. cm. — (Superchef)
Includes index.
Summary: Introduces the different culinary regions of China through recipes adapted for young chefs and discusses the basics of food handling and kitchen safety.
  ISBN 0-7614-1214-X
  1. Cookery, Chinese. I. Title. II. Series.
  TX724.5.C5 L5942 2002
  641.5951—dc21
                            2001008742

Photo Research by Rose Corbett Gordon, Mystic, CT
Photo Credits: p. 12: Keren Su/Stone/Getty Images; p. 13: Keren Su/Stone/Getty Images; p. 14: Keren Su/Stone/Getty Images; p. 15: Yannz Layma/Stone/Getty Images.
Printed in Italy
    3   5   6   4   2

Contents

DEAR READER,

I WILL ALWAYS REMEMBER THE AROMA OF ONIONS, CELERY, AND BELL PEPPER COOKING IN MY MOTHER'S CAST-IRON DUTCH OVEN. THAT APPETIZING AROMA PERMEATES MY CHILDHOOD MEMORIES AS IT DID OUR HOME. ONE OF THE MOST DELIGHTFUL THINGS I HAVE LEARNED AS A CHEF IS HOW DEEPLY FOOD INFLUENCES OUR LIVES. FOOD TOUCHES PEOPLE ON SO MANY LEVELS—PHYSICALLY, EMOTIONALLY, SOCIALLY, AND SPIRITUALLY. THE PUBLIC'S INTEREST IN FOOD AND CUISINE IS INSATIABLE, AND I AM CONSTANTLY AMAZED AT THE LEVEL OF INTEREST AND KNOWLEDGE I SEE IN YOUNG PEOPLE. THE CUISINES OF THE WORLD ARE WIDE AND VARIED AND GIVE US A GOOD PICTURE OF HUMAN NATURE AT ITS BEST. A STUDY OF THE WORLD'S MANY DIFFERENT CUISINES UNVEILS THE RICH TAPESTRY OF CULTURAL DIFFERENCES, YET IN THE END WE LEARN ONE OF LIFE'S MOST VALUABLE LESSONS: FOOD BRINGS PEOPLE TOGETHER.

THESE COOKBOOKS, WHICH I HEARTILY ENDORSE, GIVE YOUNG PEOPLE THE CHANCE TO EXPLORE, TO CREATE, AND TO LEARN. IN **Superchef**, YOUNG READERS CAN USE THEIR HOME KITCHENS TO EXPLORE THE MANY DIFFERENT TASTES OF THE WORLD. THEY CAN LEARN THE VALUE OF WORKING TOGETHER WITH FAMILY MEMBERS IN THE HOME AND EXPERIENCE THE SHEER PLEASURE OF A PERFECT MEAL. WHEN THE CUTTING, CHOPPING, AND COOKING ARE OVER, IT'S TIME TO SIT DOWN TOGETHER AND ENJOY THE FRUITS OF THE ASPIRING CHEF'S LABOR. THIS IS WHEN YOUNG CHEFS CAN LEARN THE **REAL** SECRET OF THE GREAT CHEFS—THE JOY OF SHARING.

CHEF FRANK BRIGTSEN

BRIGTSEN'S RESTAURANT
NEW ORLEANS, LOUISIANA

From the Author

Welcome to **Superchef**. This series of cookbooks brings you traditional recipes from other countries, adapted to work in your kitchen. My goal is to introduce you to a world of exciting and satisfying recipes, along with the basic principles of kitchen safety, food handling, and common-sense nutrition. Inside you will find classic recipes from China. The recipes are not necessarily all low-fat or low-calorie, but they are all healthful. Even if you are a vegetarian, you will find recipes without meat or with suggestions to make the dish meatless.

Many people today eat lots of fast food and processed or convenience foods because these are "quick and easy." As a result there are many people both young and old who simply don't know how to cook and have never experienced the pleasure of preparing a successful meal. **Superchef** can change the way you feel about cooking. You can learn to make authentic and delicious dishes from recipes that have been tested by young cooks in kitchens like yours. The recipes range from very basic to challenging. The instructions take you through the preparation of each dish step-by-step. Once you learn the basic techniques of the recipes, you will understand the principles of cooking fresh food successfully.

There is no better way to get to know someone than to share a meal. Today, more than ever, it is essential to understand the many cultures that share this planet. One way to really learn about a country is to know how its food tastes. You'll also be discovering the people of other countries while learning to prepare their classic recipes.

Learning to cook takes practice, patience, and common sense, but it's not nuclear science. Cooking certainly has its rewards. Just the simple act of preparing food can lift your spirits. Nothing brings family and friends together better than cooking and then sharing the meal you made. It can be fun, and you get to eat your mistakes. It can even lead to a high-paying career. Most importantly, you can be proud to say, "Oh, glad you liked it. I did it myself."

See you in the kitchen!

Matthew Locricchio

Before You Begin

A Word about Safety

Safety and common sense are the two most important ingredients in any recipe. Before you begin to make the recipes in this book, take a few minutes to master some simple kitchen safety rules.

✔ *Wash your hands first and often when you are working with food. Washing under hot water with lots of soap for twenty seconds will greatly reduce the risk of transferring bacteria from your hands to the food. Wash your hands again after you handle raw meats, poultry, fish, or tofu.*

✔ *Always start with a clean kitchen before you begin any recipe, and leave the kitchen clean when you're done.*

✔ *Ask an adult to be your assistant chef. To ensure your safety, some steps in a recipe are best done with the help of an adult, like handling pots of boiling water or hot cooking oils. Good cooking is about teamwork. With an adult assistant to help, you've got the makings of a perfect team.*

✔ *Read the entire recipe before you start to prepare it and have a clear understanding of how the recipe works. If something is not clear, ask your teammate to explain it.*

✔ *Dress the part of a chef. Wear an apron. Tie back long hair so that it's out of your food and away from open flames. Why not do what a chef does and wear a clean hat to cover your hair!*

✔ *Pot holders and hot pads are your friends. The hands they save may be your own. Use them only if they are dry. Using wet holders on a hot pot can cause a serious burn!*

✔ *Keep the handles of the pots and pans turned toward the middle of the stove. That way you won't accidentally hit them and knock over* pots of hot food. Always use pot holders to open or move a pan on the stove or in the oven.

✔ Remember to turn off the stove and oven when you are finished cooking. Sounds like a simple idea, but it's easy to forget.

BE SHARP ABOUT KNIVES

✔ A simple rule about knife safety is that your hands work as a team. One hand grips the handle and operates the knife while the other guides the food you are cutting. The hand holding the food should never come close to the blade of the knife. Keep the fingertips that hold the food slightly curved and out of the path of the blade, and use your thumb to keep the food steady. Go slowly. There is no reason to chop very fast.

✔ Always hold the knife handle with **dry** hands. If your hands are wet, the knife might slip. Work on a cutting board, never a tabletop or countertop.

✔ Never place sharp knives in a sink full of soapy water, where they could be hidden from view. Someone reaching into the water might get hurt.

✔ Take good care of your knives. Good chef knives should be washed by hand, never in a dishwasher.

COOKING TERMS

The first thing to remember about Chinese cooking is that the chopping and preparation of the ingredients can take longer than the actual cooking. Take the time to read the recipes carefully and to organize all of the ingredients ahead of time. The Chinese chef is a master of organization.

Be patient. Good food can take some practice to get right, so don't be discouraged if your recipe doesn't seem perfect on the first try.

Pan-fry   *This is a way to fry food in small amounts of oil. Pan-frying will brown and crisp food.*

Simmer   *Simmering means cooking over low heat just below the boiling point. It is a great technique for giving lots of flavor to dishes that require a long cooking time.*

Stir-fry   *The Chinese invented the technique of stir-frying for a very good reason: to save fuel. Chinese chefs did not have unlimited amounts of cooking fuel thousands of years ago, so they created some basic rules for cooking that still work perfectly today. Stir-frying is a simple cooking technique. But a successful stir-fry is not something that just happens. It takes planning and preparation. If you stick to the rules, the rewards are huge!*

• **Cut the main ingredients into fairly small pieces as described in the recipe. Cut them so that they are all about the same size. That way everything will cook more evenly and be done at the same time.**

- After you have cut, sliced, minced, or chopped the ingredients, line them up near the wok in the order that you will use them. When you start to stir-fry, there is no time to run around the kitchen looking for tools and ingredients. Have everything that you need ready, so when you start to cook, you won't have to look!

- Preheat your wok★ for about thirty seconds on high or medium-high heat (to be sure that the food cooks evenly). Then add the oil. Many recipes follow with garlic or ginger, for flavoring.

- The main ingredients, such as the meat or fish, usually go in next. They will make a sizzling noise as they come in contact with the hot cooking surface. Use a long-handled metal spoon or Chinese spatula to move the ingredients around. After the main ingredients are almost completely cooked, remove them and reheat the wok. Next, stir-fry the vegetables. The vegetables that need more time to cook are added first and those that need less time are added last. Green beans or carrots, for example, take longer to cook than green onions or spinach.

- Now add the seasonings and the cooking liquids such as chicken, beef, or vegetable stock.

- Some recipes call for adding cornstarch, dissolved in a liquid, at the end. It thickens and finishes the dish.

★Note: If you don't have a wok, you can use a ten- or twelve-inch frying pan with a cover instead. It will work just as well for all the recipes in this book.

The Regions of China and How They Taste

Good food brings families and friends together all over the world. In China sharing food is the very heart and soul of cooking. Rarely would anyone in China think of eating, either at home or in a restaurant, without inviting someone to share the meal. In fact, instead of saying, "Hi, how are you?" a Chinese person often will greet you with "Have you eaten yet?" If the answer is no, chances are you'll soon find yourself enjoying a delicious Chinese meal.

China is a vast country with a great variety of climates. As a result the foods grown and the ingredients used in cooking change from region to region. The best way to understand the different styles of Chinese cooking is to take a look at the main geographic areas of the country.

THE NORTHERN REGION

China's northern region includes all the lands north of the Yangtze River. Northern-style cooking is the most varied in China. Foods range from simple home-style dishes to elaborate recipes created for the imperial rulers of the ancient Chinese empire.

The northern region has much less rainfall than the rest of China and is known for its extremes in temperature. Vast plains stretch across the north, bordered by mountain ranges and flat-topped plateaus. In the plains of Manchuria, in the northeast, winter sends temperatures plummeting below zero and the ground can stay frozen eight months a year. The north is also home to the Gobi Desert, with its cold winters, short hot summers, and arid climate.

The Chinese farmer has to be very resourceful to overcome all these conditions. By controlling the river waters, building terraces in the highlands, and using intensive agriculture, farmers coax the land into producing an amazing variety of fruits, nuts, and vegetables. The cold and dry climate makes it nearly impossible to grow rice. Wheat is raised instead. Farmers also raise chickens and ducks for food. The province of Shandong, with its long coastline along the Yellow Sea, provides the region with delicious seafood.

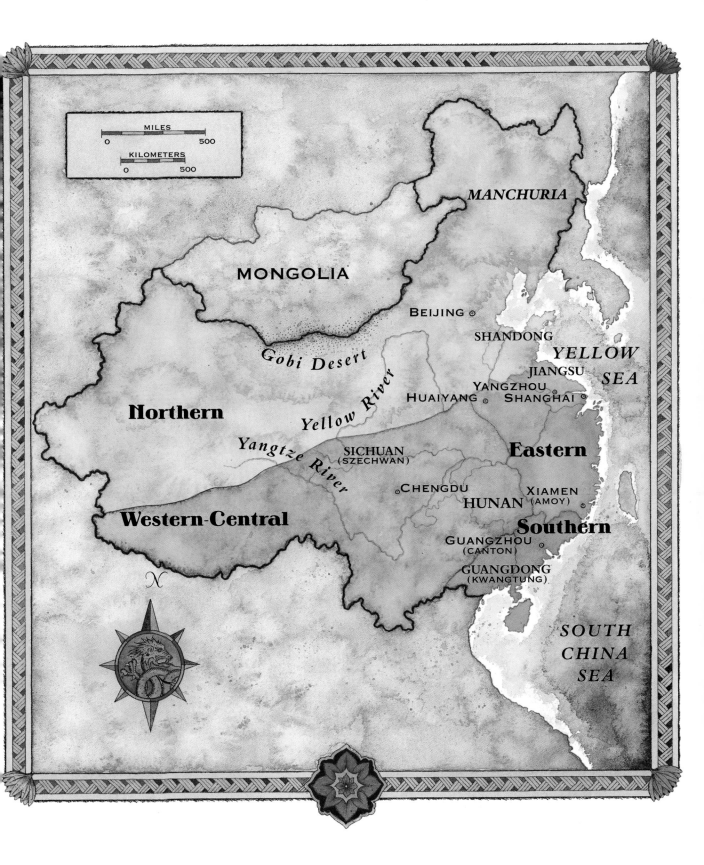

A busy outdoor vegetable market provides cooks with a bountiful selection of fresh ingredients.

Some of the most famous recipes of northern China come from Beijing. Because it is the nation's capital, Beijing has always enjoyed the best foods and the best chefs from every province in China. The Forbidden City still stands in the heart of the city. This huge walled complex of ancient buildings was home to twenty-four different emperors over the course of nearly five hundred years. Each emperor had his own chef, who created legendary dishes just for the imperial table. The classic dish Peking Duck is one famous example.

The cooking of the north tends to be less spicy than China's other regions, yet the dishes are still sharp and flavorful. Noodles and dumplings, baked buns and spring rolls, as well as lots of sweet-and-sour dishes are found here. Northern cooks use soy sauce, sesame oil, garlic, green onions, ginger, and sweet bean paste to achieve subtle flavors. For a taste of northern-style cooking, try: Hot and Sour Soup and Stir-Fried Beef Wraps with Smoked Tofu.

THE WESTERN-CENTRAL REGION

The western-central region includes Szechwan and Hunan, two of China's oldest provinces. This region is sometimes called the Land of Abundance. The climate is hot and humid, and the soil rich and fertile.

Szechwan is a scenic land of massive mountains with forbidding cliffs and deep valleys. Its high bamboo forests are home to the endangered giant panda. More than eighty rivers cross through the province. Most of Szechwan's crops are grown in the plains around the region's capital city, Chengdu, where water is supplied by a vast irrigation system built more than two thousand years ago. Southeast of Szechwan, the province of Hunan has a very different landscape. Green valleys, rich soil, lots of rainfall, and gently sloping hills and plains make Hunan the ideal place for growing plenty of rice, fruits, and vegetables.

Western-central cooking is spicy, pungent, and flavorful. Some but not all of the dishes are hot. Rice is eaten at every meal. The cooks of Hunan often preserve vegetables by pickling or marinating them. Then they mix them with the province's abundant meats, fish, and chicken. In Szechwan cooks create flavorful combinations of green onions, garlic, ginger, tofu, and nuts, as well as pork, beef, chicken, and duck. The famous Szechwan pepper comes from this region. It is often called flower pepper because the flavor seems to grow—or "flower"—in your mouth. Some Westerners stay away from Szechwan cooking because they are afraid it is too hot, but if you let yourself experiment, you may find that you really like what you taste.

The people of Szechwan and Hunan are proud of the freshness and flavor of their cuisine. This region offers some of the tastiest and healthiest dishes in Chinese cooking. The food is down-to-earth and meant to be shared. Favorite home-style dishes are called *jia-chang-cai,* which means "dishes often eaten at home." For a taste of Hunan and Szechwan cooking, try: Beggar's Chicken, Stir-Fried Orange Chicken, Ginger Beef with Green Beans, and Cold Sesame Noodles.

Terraced fields bloom in the rich soil of China's Land of Abundance.

The picturesque beauty of a mountain village is typical of the sights that draw visitors to eastern China.

THE EASTERN REGION

Marco Polo, the thirteenth-century Italian explorer, called China's eastern region a "heavenly paradise." Today eastern China is still a favorite tourist destination, not only for its beauty but also for its food. The climate is the most moderate in China. Rainfall is abundant. The winters are mild and the soil is fertile, producing an abundance of crops, including bamboo shoots, beans, rice, sweet corn, soybeans, peaches, plums, melons, and grapes. Eastern cooks have made good use of the land's bounty, developing outstanding vegetarian recipes.

The area also serves up great freshwater fish and seafood. The chefs of Shanghai, a bustling port city of more than thirteen million people, have absorbed cooking influences from all over China and the world. Seafood recipes from Shanghai are considered some of the best in the country.

Vinegars and condiments, especially soy sauce, from the eastern region are prized all across China. One favorite—dark and pungent Chinkiang vinegar—is often used in dipping sauces.

The cooking of eastern China combines the fresh tastes in the main ingredients with the sweet and rich flavors in the sauce. For a taste of eastern-style cooking, try Fried Rice.

THE SOUTHERN REGION

Southern China gave the Western world its first taste of Chinese cooking. Immigrants from the southern port city of Guangzhou (Canton) brought their distinctive cooking style with them wherever they went. They introduced Cantonese cooking to the United States in the nineteenth century, when they came to build the railroads. Today Cantonese cooking is still very popular all over the world.

The southern region is known as China's rice bowl because its climate is ideal for growing rice. The warm temperatures, frequent rainfall, and rich soil also produce a great variety of fruits and vegetables, including black mushrooms, green onions, bok choy, bananas, pineapples, oranges, and litchi nuts. The South China Sea adds plenty of fresh seafood to the menu.

In the southern kitchen you will find garlic, black bean sauce, oyster sauce, garlic sauce, fresh ginger, and soy sauce. Stir-frying and sautéing are an art here. The chef is very careful to cut everything into uniform pieces so the ingredients will cook quickly and evenly. The Cantonese are especially known for their barbecued pork and crispy-skin duck.

The people of southern China believe that there is no better place to visit if you really love good food. Southern-style cooking is considered the most highly developed in China. It uses the greatest assortment of ingredients, in fancy dishes that emphasize color, texture, and fresh, natural flavors. For a taste of southern-style cooking, try: Velvet Corn Soup, Sweet-and-Sour Tofu Stir-Fry, Stir-Fried Shrimp and Red Peppers, Egg Rolls, and the famous dessert Almond Cookies.

With Grandmother's help, a child enjoys eating a bowl of noodles.

The Basics

Homemade Chicken Stock (page 18),
Homemade Vegetable Stock (page 20),
and Chinese White Rice (page 23)

Homemade Chicken Stock *Jia Chang Ji Tang*

Broth is the liquid in which chicken, meat, fish, or vegetables have been cooked; when that liquid is used as the base for soup or a sauce, it is called stock. A good stock is the foundation for great flavor. Great flavor is what making your own chicken stock is all about. Of course, you can buy chicken stock in a can. But once you make your own, you may never go back to canned again. This recipe makes ½ gallon of stock.

Ingredients

3 to 4 pounds chicken (preferably organic), cut into 8 pieces
3 slices fresh ginger
3 whole green onions
1 stalk celery, cut into large chunks

1 onion, cut into quarters
2 carrots, cut into large chunks
1 tablespoon salt (optional)
10 cups cold water (2 ½ quarts)

On your mark, get set . . .

- Wash the chicken under cold running water. Wash the work area where the chicken was cleaned.
- Peel the ginger. Crush the ginger and green onions with the flat side of a knife.

Cook!

- Place all the ingredients in a large pot.
- Bring to a boil, then reduce the heat to low and simmer for about 1 ½ hours. A white foam will rise to the surface as the liquid cooks. With a large spoon, carefully remove the foam and discard. As the stock cooks, continue to remove any additional foam that rises to the surface.
- After it has cooked, turn off the heat. Ask your adult assistant to help you strain the stock through a colander lined with cheesecloth. Discard the chicken and vegetables (although the chicken is pretty tasty as a snack).
- Allow the stock to cool, uncovered, for about 20 minutes. Then cover it and refrigerate. The white fat that will separate and rise to the top of the stock after it has cooled should be removed and discarded. You now have pure chicken stock!

What Does "Organic" Mean?

Organic fruits and vegetables are grown without the use of chemical pesticides or chemical fertilizers and as a result produce a product that has much less impact on the environment. Organic poultry and meats are raised without the use of antibiotics or growth hormones. Many people believe that organic products are healthier for you and taste better than non-organic products. If organic chickens and produce are available in your area, why not try them and see if they really do taste better? As a rule, organic products are expensive, so keep your budget in mind when you are shopping.

Chef's Tip

The finished chicken stock will keep for up to one week in the refrigerator in an airtight container, or it can be poured into smaller plastic containers with tight-fitting lids and frozen for up to three months. To thaw, place the container upside down under cold running water and press the bottom to push out the frozen stock. Heat the stock in a covered pan on low heat until it melts. Chicken stock can also be thawed overnight in the refrigerator. Never thaw chicken stock on the counter or at room temperature.

Homemade Vegetable Stock
Jia Chang Su Cai Tang

Just like chicken stock, vegetable stock can be bought in cans, but give this recipe a try and see how good the real thing can taste! This recipe makes ½ gallon of stock.

Ingredients

6 carrots
3 stalks celery
1 yellow onion, cut into quarters
3 green onions
6 leaves iceberg lettuce (or your choice of lettuce)

3 slices fresh ginger, about ½ inch thick
    and the size of a quarter
½ pound fresh mushrooms (optional)
1 tablespoon salt (optional)
10 cups cold water (2 ½ quarts)

On your mark, get set . . .

- **Wash all the vegetables. Wipe off any dirt from the mushrooms with a dry paper towel. You don't have to peel the carrots or the onions—the skins will give the stock extra flavor.**
- **Chop the vegetables into large chunks.**

Cook!

- **Place all the ingredients in a large pot.**
- **Bring to a boil over high heat, then reduce the heat to low and simmer for 1 ½ hours. With a large spoon, remove any foam that rises to the surface of the liquid as it cooks. Discard the foam.**
- **When the stock has finished cooking, turn off the heat. Ask your adult assistant to help you pour it through a colander lined with cheesecloth. Discard the vegetables.**
- **Let the stock cool, uncovered, for 20 minutes, then cover and refrigerate.**

CHEF'S TIP

Vegetable stock can be refrigerated in an airtight container for up to seven days. It can also be frozen in smaller plastic containers with tight-fitting lids for up to three months. To thaw, place the container upside down under cold running water and press the bottom to push out the frozen stock. Place the stock in a pan on the stove. Heat, covered, on low heat until the stock melts. It can also be thawed overnight in the refrigerator. Never thaw vegetable stock on the counter or at room temperature.

THE STORY OF RICE

RICE IS THE MOST COMMON GRAIN in the world today. It feeds more people than any other grain and is cultivated in more than 110 countries. Rice is consumed every day, in one form or another, by half the world's population and has been for thousands of years.

The first rice fields were cultivated in the Yangtze River Valley in China more than eight thousand years ago. Chinese farmers still grow rice using ancient farming methods, because these methods do the best job of producing good rice.

Rice plays a big role in Chinese culture. It is part of the folklore of the nation. The Chinese believe it is bad luck to tip over a rice bowl. The biggest insult you can pay a person is to throw his or her rice bowl on the ground. Rice remains a sign of a prosperous and rewarding life. It is thrown at weddings as a symbol of good luck. In some regions of China, a wooden bowl of rice is offered as a remembrance on the altars of relatives who have died.

The Chinese generally like their rice plain because it often accompanies food that is hot and spicy. Rice goes well with meat, fish, and vegetables. Its flavor is plain and simple, and the other flavors in a dish blend together with it perfectly.

There are several types of rice you can choose from. Short grain rice is the smallest. It tends to be sticky and starchy. Short grain rice is great for desserts like rice pudding. Medium grain rice is a little fatter and less starchy. Long grain and extra long grain rice are the most popular in China and are recommended for the recipes in this book.

You can also buy converted rice, which takes less time to cook because it is pre-cooked. Apart from white rice, there is brown rice. Brown rice still has the outer coating that is polished away to yield white rice. While brown rice is highly nutritious, it is less popular in China than white rice.

After you open a bag of rice, it is best to store it in a canister or a glass jar with a tight-fitting lid. Keep it dry and it will stay fresh for a very long time.

Rice is the easiest food in the world to cook. You can steam it, boil it, or fry it. Electric rice cookers, which are becoming more popular in China—and in the United States as well—than ever before, do a great job of steaming rice.

Next time you see that tiny grain of rice, think about how many people it can feed and how many centuries it has been cultivated on earth. But most of all, think how delicious it is going to taste with that wonderful stir-fry you are about to make.

Chinese White Rice *Bai Mi Fan*

The most basic part of any Chinese meal is the rice. There are many different types of rice you can buy. For the recipes in this book, long grain or extra long grain rice is recommended. You can follow the directions on the package, or try this authentic recipe.

Serves 6

Ingredients

1 cup extra long grain white rice
1 3/4 cups water
1 teaspoon salt (optional)

On your mark . . .

- Pour the rice into a hand strainer.
- Rinse under cold running water a minute or two to remove the starch. Using a chopstick, a spoon, or your fingers, stir the rice as you rinse it. You will know the rice is ready to cook when the water running out of the strainer is clear.

Get set . . .

- Place the rice and salt in a 2-quart saucepan and add 1 3/4 cups water.
- Let the rice and water stand, uncovered, for at least 10 minutes or up to an hour. This will help to soften the rice.

Cook!

- Place the rice over high heat. Bring to a full boil. Continue to cook for 1 minute on high heat.
- Cover the pan, reduce the heat to the lowest setting, and cook for 20 minutes. Don't be tempted to lift the lid and peek at the cooking rice.
- After 20 minutes, turn off the heat and let the rice rest on the burner for 10 minutes.
- When ready to serve, stir with a chopstick or spoon to loosen the grains and fluff the rice.

Soups & Appetizers

Clockwise from top:
Egg Rolls (page 34),
Fried Rice (page 30),
Chilled Cucumber and Sesame Salad (page 37),
and Cold Sesame Noodles (page 33)

Velvet Corn Soup *Yu Mi Geng*

This Cantonese recipe has been made in China for hundreds of years. While it was originally prepared with fresh corn from the fields, this version uses creamed corn and smoked ham. This soup is easy to make and very satisfying on a cold day. Try serving it as a first course before your favorite stir-fried dish.

Serves 4-6

Ingredients

1 medium-size boneless skinless chicken breast (about 4 ounces), preferably organic
1/4 pound smoked ham or Smithfield ham
2 egg whites
1 teaspoon salt
2 cups creamed corn

4 cups low-sodium chicken stock (home-made or canned)
1 tablespoon cornstarch, mixed with 2 tablespoons water
2 green onions, finely chopped

On your mark . . .

- **Place the chicken breast in the freezer for 20 to 30 minutes. Partially freezing it will make it easier to cut.**
- **Slice the ham into long strips, then into 1/2-inch cubes, and refrigerate.**

Get set . . .

- **Slice the chicken into long strips, then into cubes slightly larger than the ham.**
- **Using an electric hand mixer, beat the egg whites until they are almost stiff.**
- **Add the chicken cubes and salt to the egg whites and refrigerate.**
- **Wash the beaters of the hand mixer. Beat the creamed corn with the electric mixer for about 30 seconds, or until smooth.**

Cook!

- **In a 4-quart pot, bring the chicken stock to a boil.**
- **Line up these ingredients on your countertop: chicken mixture, creamed corn, cornstarch mixture, ham cubes, green onions.**
- **Add the chicken mixture and creamed corn to the chicken stock. Slowly bring the soup back to a boil. This will take 2 to 3 minutes.**
- **Stir the cornstarch and water mixture to recombine. When the soup boils, stir in the cornstarch.**
- **Add the ham cubes and cook for another minute, stirring, to finish the soup.**
- **Serve hot, with the chopped green onions sprinkled on top, and pass the soy sauce at the table.**

Hot and Sour Soup *Suan La Tang*

This is one of the most recognizable soups in Chinese cooking. It is said to have originated in Beijing, though the Szechwan and Hunan cooks in China insist this dish comes from their provinces. Once you try your own homemade version, you will want to claim it as your own dish, too. If you can't find dried shiitake mushrooms, you can substitute fresh ones. Just follow the note at the end of the recipe. The white pepper gives the soup its heat, so you can add more or less of it as you like.

Serves 6

Ingredients

4 dried shiitake mushrooms
1/4 pound boneless pork loin, slightly frozen
3 ounces firm tofu
1 green onion
1/2 cup bamboo shoots
4 cups low-sodium chicken stock (homemade or canned)
1 teaspoon salt

2 teaspoons soy sauce
1/4 teaspoon ground white pepper (optional)
2 tablespoons white vinegar
1/2 cup frozen sweet peas
2 tablespoons cornstarch mixed with 3 tablespoons water
1 egg, slightly beaten
1 teaspoon sesame oil

On your mark . . .

- Soak the dried mushrooms in 1/2 cup warm water for 20 to 30 minutes.*
- Cut the pork into thin slices. Stack the slices of pork a few at a time and cut into slivers.
- Cut the tofu into long strips and then into 2-inch squares.
- Finely chop the green onion.
- Rinse the bamboo shoots in a hand strainer under cold running water to remove any bitter taste. Then cut them into thin slices.

Get set . . .

- Drain the mushrooms, saving the liquid. Using a pair of kitchen scissors, cut off the stems and discard. Cut the mushroom caps into thin slices.
- Line up these ingredients on your countertop: chicken stock, mushroom liquid, pork, salt, soy sauce, mushrooms, bamboo shoots, tofu, white pepper, vinegar, frozen peas, cornstarch mixture, egg, green onion, sesame oil.

Cook!

- Pour the chicken stock and mushroom liquid into a 4-quart pot.
- Add the pork, salt, soy sauce, mushrooms, and bamboo shoots. Bring to a boil over high heat. Then reduce the heat to low, cover, and simmer for 5 minutes.
- Add the tofu, white pepper, vinegar, and frozen peas. Raise the heat to high and bring the soup back to a boil.
- Stir the cornstarch and water to recombine and slowly pour into the boiling soup. Gently stir the soup for a few seconds as it thickens.
- Carefully stir in the egg and cook for 30 seconds.
- Turn off the heat and add the green onion and sesame oil. Stir and serve hot in bowls.

CHEF'S TIP

To make this soup vegetarian: Omit the pork and egg; use vegetable stock instead of chicken stock; use 6 ounces tofu, 2 green onions, and 2 teaspoons of salt.

★Note: If you can't find dried shiitake mushrooms, you can substitute fresh mushrooms. Look for fresh shiitake or small Portobello mushrooms. Remove and discard the stems, brush any dirt from the mushrooms with a dry paper towel, and slice the mushroom caps before adding to the pot. It is not necessary to soak fresh mushrooms, so you can omit the mushroom liquid from the recipe.

Fried Rice *Chao Fan*

Fried rice is one of the most popular dishes in Chinese cooking. It is a great way to use leftover rice and turn it into a fast and delicious meal or the perfect side dish. The story goes that this dish was first created in the city of Yangzhou, in the eastern province of Jiangsu.

Serves 6

Ingredients

3 cups cold cooked white rice
1/4 pound fresh or frozen shrimp (if frozen, thaw before using)
3 extra-large eggs
1 cup diced roast pork or cooked ham
3 green onions
3 tablespoons canola or peanut oil

Sauce

1 tablespoon soy sauce
1/2 tablespoon oyster sauce
1 teaspoon sugar
1 teaspoon sesame oil
1 teaspoon minced fresh ginger
1/2 teaspoon salt

On your mark . . .

- **Prepare the rice and chill it. If using leftover rice, separate any clumps with your fingers. This works best if your hands are wet. Measure 3 cups.**
- **Peel the shrimp and discard the shells. Cut the shrimp in half lengthwise. Rinse under cold running water, and pull out the vein and discard. Cut the shrimp into small pieces and refrigerate.**
- **Break the eggs into a bowl and lightly scramble with a fork.**
- **Dice the pork or ham by cutting it first into strips, then into 1/2-inch pieces. Measure 1 cup.**
- **Slice the green onions into 1/4-inch pieces.**
- **Measure 3 tablespoons canola oil and set aside.**
- **Combine the ingredients for the sauce with a spoon and set aside.**

Get set . . .

- **Line up these ingredients on your countertop: canola oil, eggs, shrimp, rice, sauce, roast pork or ham, green onions.**

Cook!

- Heat a wok on medium-high heat for 30 seconds. Add the eggs and cook for 1 minute, breaking them up with a spatula into very small pieces. Remove the eggs to a small bowl.

- Scrape out the wok and place it back on the stove over medium-high heat. Add 1 tablespoon of the canola oil and heat for 30 seconds.
- Add the shrimp and cook for 2 minutes. The shrimp should be bright pink when cooked. Remove the shrimp.
- Add the remaining 2 tablespoons of oil and reheat the wok for 30 seconds. Add the rice. Using the spatula, spread the rice around the wok to make sure all the grains get as much heat as possible. Cook for about 1 minute.
- Add the sauce and mix well, coating all the rice. Cook for 2 minutes, stirring constantly.
- Add the shrimp, eggs, roast pork or ham, and green onions. Combine all the ingredients, using the spatula. Cook for another minute or two, or until everything is hot. Serve hot.

Cold Sesame Noodles *Liang Mian*

This recipe comes from the provinces of Hunan and Szechwan. The weather there gets hot and sticky in the summer months, and cold dishes are just the right thing for a refreshing summer meal. Cold Sesame Noodles can start a meal, make a wonderful lunch, or be served as part of a large banquet. Any way you serve it, this dish will be asked for again and again. If you wish to make the noodles vegetarian, use vegetable stock instead of chicken stock.

Serves 6

Ingredients

1/2 pound angel hair pasta
1 tablespoon sesame oil

Dressing

1/2 cup chunky peanut butter
1/2 cup low-sodium chicken or vegetable
   stock (homemade or canned)
3 tablespoons soy sauce
2 tablespoons sesame oil
1 tablespoon Worcestershire sauce
1 tablespoon sugar
1/2 teaspoon ground white pepper

Topping

1 green onion
1/4 cup chopped peanuts
2 tablespoons sesame seeds

On your mark, get set, cook!

- Cook the pasta according to the package directions. Drain in a colander, then toss with 1 tablespoon sesame oil. Refrigerate for at least 1 hour.
- Place the ingredients for the dressing in a quart jar with a lid, and shake until well blended. Refrigerate until ready to serve.
- Mince the green onion, measure about 1/4 cup, and refrigerate.
- Measure out the chopped peanuts, and toast the sesame seeds in an oven or a toaster oven 4 to 5 minutes.
- To serve, arrange the cold pasta on a serving platter. Pour the dressing over the pasta and sprinkle the green onion, chopped peanuts, and sesame seeds over the top.

Egg Rolls *Chun Juan*

Egg rolls, a creation from Canton, are actually part of a delicious collection of appetizers called dim sum. This recipe is made without deep-frying. Instead, the egg rolls are pan-fried. They are light, delicious, and really fun to make.

Serves 12

Ingredients

½ pound fresh or frozen shrimp
   (if frozen, thaw before using)
½ small head cabbage
1 stalk celery
3 green onions
2 slices fresh ginger, unpeeled
1 clove garlic, unpeeled
8 cups cold water (2 quarts)

1 tablespoon sugar
4 teaspoons salt
½ cup canola oil
1 tablespoon soy sauce
1 teaspoon sesame oil
12 egg roll or spring roll wrappers
1 egg, slightly beaten
1 cup bean sprouts

On your mark ...

- **Peel the shrimp and discard the shells. Cut the shrimp in half lengthwise. Rinse under cold running water, and pull out the vein and discard. Refrigerate the cut shrimp.**
- Cut the cabbage into thin slices and measure 2 cups.
- Cut the celery into ¼-inch pieces.
- Cut the green onions into ¼-inch pieces.
- Using the flat side of a knife, crush the slices of ginger and the garlic.
- Fill a large pot with 8 cups water and add the ginger and garlic.
- Add the sugar and 2 teaspoons of the salt. Cover and bring to a boil.
- Add the shrimp and cook, uncovered, for 1 minute, or just until the shrimp turn pink. Using a slotted spoon or Chinese strainer, remove the shrimp and place them in a colander. After the shrimp are drained, place them in a large bowl.
- Remove the ginger and garlic from the water and discard.
- Bring the same pot of water back to a boil and add the cabbage and celery. Cook for 1 to 2 minutes, or until the cabbage is bright green.
- Drain the vegetables into a colander. Using the back of a large slotted spoon, press down on the cabbage and celery to remove any extra water. Give the colander a few gentle tosses to remove the last of the water. Then add the cabbage and celery to the shrimp.

Get set . . .

- Heat a wok on medium-high heat for 1 minute. Add 1 tablespoon of the canola oil. Heat for 30 seconds.
- Add the sliced green onions and stir-fry for 1 minute.
- Now add the shrimp and vegetable mixture, soy sauce, sesame oil, and the remaining 2 teaspoons salt. Stir-fry for 1 minute, mixing all the ingredients together.
- Empty the stir-fry ingredients into a colander to drain. These ingredients are the filling for the egg rolls.
- On a clean surface, lay out 1 egg roll wrapper as if it were a baseball diamond. Home plate is the corner facing you. Cover the rest of the wrappers so they won't dry out.
- Using a pastry brush, paint a little of the beaten egg all along the outside edge of the wrapper.
- Place about 1 1/2 tablespoons of the filling in a line between first and third base. Add a small bunch of the bean sprouts on top of the filling.
- Beginning at home plate, roll up halfway, gently packing the filling inside. Tuck the first- and third-base corners into the center and finish rolling to second base. You just made an egg roll!
- Place on a platter, cover with plastic wrap, and keep cold while you make the rest. Repeat until all the egg rolls are made.

Cook!

- **Preheat the oven to 200°F.**
- Heat 2 tablespoons of the canola oil in a wok or frying pan for about 30 seconds.
- Using a pair of tongs to lift and turn the egg rolls, carefully pan-fry them—1 at a time in a wok or 2 at a time in a frying pan—until they are golden brown and crispy. This will take about 2 to 3 minutes each. Add the remaining oil to the pan as needed.
- Let the finished egg rolls drain on paper towels. Then keep them warm in the oven until all of them are ready.
- Serve hot with a dipping sauce.

DIPPING SAUCES

Duck Sauce and Vinegar
2 tablespoons duck sauce
1 tablespoon rice wine vinegar

Soy and Ginger
1 tablespoon soy sauce
1 teaspoon fresh ginger, minced, or chopped very finely
1 tablespoon sesame oil

CHEF'S TIP

To make the egg rolls vegetarian, omit the shrimp and use spring roll wrappers. Spring roll wrappers are more fragile than egg roll wrappers because they are made without eggs. Handle them carefully so they won't tear.

Chilled Cucumber and Sesame Salad

Liang Ban La Huang Gua

This recipe is a great example of how simple Chinese cooking can be. Chilled cucumbers in a tasty sesame dressing make a perfect salad that can be enjoyed both summer and winter.

Serves 4

Ingredients

Salad

2 cucumbers
1 head green leaf lettuce

Dressing

1 tablespoon balsamic vinegar
1 tablespoon sugar
1 tablespoon chunky peanut butter

1 teaspoon soy sauce
1 teaspoon sesame oil
1 teaspoon sea salt

On your mark . . .

- Wash and peel the cucumbers. Place them on a cutting board and cut them in half lengthwise. Using a teaspoon, start at one end and scrape out the seeds. Discard the seeds.
- Slice the cucumbers into 1/4-inch chunks. Measure about 2 1/2 cups and place in a medium-size glass bowl.
- Wash and pat dry the lettuce leaves. Tear the lettuce into bite-size pieces, arrange on a serving platter, and refrigerate.

Get set . . .

- For the dressing: In a small bowl, mix together all the ingredients. Make sure the peanut butter blends well into the dressing. This may take some time.

Toss!

- Pour the dressing over the cucumber chunks and gently toss with a fork. Refrigerate the cucumbers until they are cold.
- When you are ready to serve the salad, spoon the cucumbers over the lettuce.

Vegetable Dishes

Sweet-and-Sour Tofu Stir-Fry (page 42) and Stir-Fried Green Beans and Green Onions (page 41) served with rice

Stir-Fried Green Beans and Green Onions

Qiang Chao Si Ji Dou

Green beans and green onions come together beautifully in this vegetarian dish that is packed with flavor and easy to make. Try it along with Sweet-and-Sour Tofu Stir-Fry (page 42) or Beggar's Chicken (page 56), or as a cold salad.

Serves 6

Ingredients

2 slices fresh ginger
1 clove garlic
12 ounces fresh green beans
1 carrot
3 green onions

2 tablespoons peanut oil
1 teaspoon salt
1 teaspoon sugar
2 tablespoons water
1 tablespoon sesame oil

On your mark . . .

- Peel the ginger and cut into 1/4-inch pieces. Crush the ginger with the flat side of a large knife or use a garlic press.
- Crush the garlic and remove the skin.
- Wash the green beans, drain, and cut in half.
- Wash, peel, and cut the carrot in half lengthwise and then cut into strips about the same size as the green beans.
- Wash the green onions, and slice them into 1/2-inch pieces.

Get set . . .

- Line up these ingredients on your countertop: peanut oil, ginger, garlic, green beans, carrot, salt, sugar, water, green onions, sesame oil.

Cook!

- Heat a wok on medium-high heat for 30 seconds. Add the peanut oil.
- After a few seconds, add the crushed ginger and garlic. Stir-fry for 30 seconds to flavor the oil. Remove the ginger and garlic with a long-handled spoon or Chinese spatula and discard.
- Add the green beans and carrot, and stir-fry for 1 minute.
- Add the salt, sugar, and water. Cover and reduce the heat to low. Cook for 2 to 3 minutes.
- Remove the lid and return the heat to medium-high. Add the green onions and sesame oil, and stir-fry for another minute.
- Serve hot with rice.

Sweet-and-Sour Tofu Stir-Fry

Tian Suan Dou Fu

Sweet-and-sour flavors are essential elements in the cooking of China. This dish is a tasty sampling of Cantonese cooking. It is filled with flavor, and the tofu provides lots of protein. Tofu continues to grow more and more popular in Western kitchens. Today many different varieties and flavors are available in the United States. Firm tofu, either plain or flavored, will work best in this dish.

Serves 6

Ingredients

8 ounces firm tofu, flavored or plain
1 small red bell pepper
1 medium-size fresh shiitake mushroom
1/4 cup bamboo shoots
4 green onions
1 tablespoon peanut oil
1/4 cup cashews

Marinade

1/4 cup fresh lemon juice
2 tablespoons ketchup
1 tablespoon dark soy sauce
1 tablespoon honey
1 1/2 teaspoons grated fresh ginger

On your mark . . .

- Cut the tofu into long strips and then into 2-inch squares, and place in a small glass bowl.
- In a separate small bowl, combine the ingredients for the marinade and mix well.
- Pour marinade over the tofu and refrigerate for at least 30 minutes or overnight. The longer the tofu marinates, the more flavor it will have.

Get set . . .

- Wash the red pepper and cut in half. Remove the stem and seeds and discard. Cut the pepper into slices and then into 1/2-inch pieces.
- Remove the stem from the mushroom and discard. Cut the mushroom cap into thin slices.
- Cut the bamboo shoots into thin slices.
- Cut the green onions into 1/4-inch sections.
- Line up these ingredients on your countertop: peanut oil, red pepper, mushroom, bamboo shoots, green onions, cashews, tofu and marinade.

Cook!

- Heat a wok on medium-high heat for 30 seconds. Add the peanut oil.
- After a few seconds, add the red pepper, mushroom, bamboo shoots, green onions, and cashews. Stir-fry for 1 minute.
- Add the tofu and marinade. Stir-fry until all the ingredients are well combined and most of the liquid has cooked away.
- Serve hot with rice.

Main Dishes

Stir-Fried Shrimp and Red Peppers
(page 54)

Stir-Fried Orange Chicken *Qiang Chao Chen Pi Ji*

Here is an adaptation of a classic Hunan recipe. This dish is usually cooked with red chili peppers, and that adds lots of heat. This version eliminates the hot peppers, but it still has great flavor. It also does not deep-fry the chicken, making it lighter in fat and calories. Try serving it with Stir-Fried Green Beans and Green Onions (page 40).

Serves 6

Ingredients

2 medium-size partially frozen,★ boneless
  skinless chicken breasts (about 10 ounces),
  preferably organic
3 tablespoons canola oil

Sauce

1 orange
1 tablespoon soy sauce
2 tablespoons hoisin sauce
1 tablespoon apple cider vinegar
1/2 teaspoon cornstarch
1/4 teaspoon ground white pepper

Marinade

2 tablespoons soy sauce
2 tablespoons balsamic vinegar
1 tablespoon water
1 teaspoon sesame oil
1 teaspoon finely chopped fresh ginger
1/2 teaspoon cornstarch

On your mark . . .

- **Wash the partially frozen chicken under cold running water and pat dry with paper towels.**
- **On a cutting board, slice the chicken into long strips and then cut into 1-inch cubes. Place the chicken cubes in a medium-size glass bowl. Wash the cutting board and knife in hot, soapy water.**

- **In a small bowl, mix together all the ingredients for the marinade. Pour over the chicken cubes and refrigerate.**

  ★Note: Partially freezing the chicken breasts makes them easier to cut; 20 to 30 minutes should be enough time in the freezer to firm them. Remember to set a timer so you don't forget them!

Get set . . .

- For the sauce: Wash the orange and dry it. Using a potato peeler, peel off 6 slices of the skin (be careful not to cut too deep into the orange). Cut the orange in half and squeeze out 1/4 cup juice. Remove any seeds that fall into the juice.

- In a small bowl, combine the juice, orange peels, soy sauce, hoisin sauce, cider vinegar, cornstarch, and white pepper. Mix well.

Cook!

- Place the sauce near the stove. Remove the marinated chicken from the refrigerator.
- Heat a wok on medium-high heat for 30 seconds. Add 1 tablespoon of the canola oil.
- After a few seconds, carefully add half the chicken cubes with about half the marinade. Spread the chicken in a single layer over the bottom of the wok and let it cook undisturbed for 2 minutes. Then give the chicken a good stir and let it cook for another 2 to 3 minutes, or until it is browned and a little crispy. Remove the chicken to a clean medium-size bowl.

- Reheat the wok for a few seconds and add another 1 tablespoon oil. Cook the rest of the chicken and marinade in the same way, removing when done.
- Reheat the wok and add the remaining 1 tablespoon oil. Using a pair of tongs, lift the orange peels out of the sauce, add them to the hot oil, and stir-fry for a few seconds.

- Give the sauce a stir and pour it into the wok.
- Add all the cooked chicken. Stir-fry for another minute or so, or until the sauce thickens.
- Serve hot over rice.

Ginger Beef with Green Beans

Cong Jiang Niu Rou

Try this recipe from the provinces of Hunan and Szechwan. After you taste it, you will see why some Chinese call Hunan and Szechwan cooking the most distinctive in China. This recipe calls for a red chili pepper. If you decide to use it, be sure to read more about handling that hot little devil in the Essential Ingredients section at the back of the book.

Serves 4

Ingredients

10 ounces fresh green beans
1 clove garlic
1 tablespoon balsamic vinegar
1/2 pound beef tenderloin
4 tablespoons peanut oil
1/2 cup dry-roasted peanuts
1 teaspoon salt
2 tablespoons soy sauce

Marinade

1 tablespoon balsamic vinegar
2 1/2 teaspoons cornstarch
1 1/2 teaspoons finely chopped fresh ginger
1 teaspoon sugar
1 green onion, cut into 1/4-inch pieces
1 whole red cayenne chili pepper, fresh or dried★ (optional)

On your mark . . .

- **Wash the green beans and string them: Start at the pointed end of the bean, pull the string down, and remove it. Cut the beans into 2-inch sections.**
- **Peel and finely chop the garlic.**
- **Mix 1 tablespoon balsamic vinegar with the garlic and pour over the beans. Set aside.**
- **Cut the beef tenderloin into thin slices. Stack the slices on top of each other a few at a time and cut them into strips. Place them in a glass bowl. Wash the knife and cutting board with hot, soapy water.**
- **In a small bowl, mix together the ingredients for the marinade. Pour over the beef strips and mix well. Refrigerate until ready to use, about 20 minutes.**

Get Set . . .

- **Line up these ingredients on your countertop: peanut oil, green beans, peanuts, salt, marinated beef, and soy sauce.**

Cook!

- Heat a wok on medium-high heat for 30 seconds. Add 2 tablespoons of the peanut oil.
- After 15 seconds, add the green beans, peanuts, and salt. Stir-fry for 3 to 4 minutes. The skin of the beans will darken and wrinkle. Remove the beans to a warm plate.
- Reheat the wok and add the remaining 2 tablespoons oil. Heat for 30 seconds.
- Add the marinated beef, a little at a time, until all the beef and marinade are added. Stir-fry for 3 to 4 minutes, using a spatula to move the beef around.
- Return the green beans to the wok. Add the soy sauce and stir-fry for another minute.
- Serve hot with rice.

*Note: If you can't find fresh or dried chili peppers, you can substitute 1/4 teaspoon cayenne pepper.

Stir-Fried Beef Wraps with Smoked Tofu
Niu Rou Dou Fu Bao

This wonderful combination of great flavors—stir-fried ground beef and rich, smoky tofu, rolled up in a delicate lettuce leaf—comes from the northern region of China. It is a great example of how creative the Chinese cook can be. If you can't find Boston/Bibb lettuce, any other lettuce will work, but the leaves of some varieties may break apart when you try to roll them. Don't worry. The stiffer lettuce leaves can work just as well: Instead of rolling the leaf, just put the filling on top and eat the Beef Wrap like a taco.

Serves 4

Ingredients

1 pound ground top round beef
2 tablespoons dark soy sauce
1 1/2 tablespoons apple cider vinegar
1 1/2 teaspoons cornstarch
12 leaves Boston/Bibb or iceberg lettuce
8 ounces firm tofu, smoked or flavored

2 tablespoons canola oil
1 cup frozen peas
2 tablespoons oyster sauce
2 teaspoons cornstarch mixed with
*   1 tablespoon water*

On your mark . . .

- **Place the ground beef in a large bowl.**
- **Add the soy sauce, cider vinegar, and 1 1/2 teaspoons cornstarch. Using very clean hands or a spoon, mix together. Wash your hands. Refrigerate the beef mixture.**
- **Wash the lettuce leaves and pat dry with a paper towel. Arrange the lettuce on a serving platter and keep cold.**
- **Cut the tofu into long strips. Using very clean hands, crumble the tofu strips into a small bowl and set aside.**

Get set . . .

- **Line up these ingredients on your countertop: canola oil, beef mixture, frozen peas, tofu, oyster sauce, cornstarch mixture.**

Cook!

- Heat a wok on medium-high heat for 30 seconds. Add the canola oil. Heat for another 30 seconds.
- Add the beef mixture and cook for 5 to 8 minutes. The liquid will disappear and the meat will change color as it cooks.
- Add the frozen peas, tofu, and oyster sauce. Stir-fry for 3 to 4 minutes.
- Stir the cornstarch and water to recombine, and add to the wok. Cook for a few more seconds, or until all the ingredients are combined. This is the filling. Transfer the filling to a warm serving bowl.
- To serve, let your guests place about 2 tablespoons of the filling in the center of each lettuce leaf and then roll it up. Beef Wraps are eaten with your fingers, like egg rolls or tacos.

Stir-Fried Shrimp and Red Peppers

Qing Jiao Xia

The southeastern region of China, including Kwangtung and its capital of Canton, has produced the most varied and popular cuisine in the country. The Cantonese are some of the most versatile cooks in all of China, and for good reason. Seafood comes from their coastal waters and fresh fish from their rivers. Their farms produce everything from prized vegetables to tropical fruits and nuts. Stir-Fried Shrimp and Red Peppers will introduce you to the popular combination of Chinese parsley, ginger, and garlic, blended with the flavor of fresh shrimp.

Serves 6

Ingredients

1 pound medium-size shrimp
1 red bell pepper
1 green onion
3 tablespoons peanut oil
Chinese parsley (cilantro), 2 tablespoons finely chopped

Marinade

2 tablespoons cornstarch
1 tablespoon soy sauce
1 tablespoon balsamic vinegar
1 teaspoon salt
1 egg white
1 clove garlic, peeled and crushed
2 slices fresh ginger (1/4 inch thick), peeled and minced

On your mark . . .

- In a small bowl, combine the ingredients for the marinade and mix well.
- Peel the shrimp and discard the shells. Take 1 shrimp and lay it flat on a cutting board. Using a paring knife, make a slight cut in the outside curve of the shrimp. You will find a black vein. Remove it by pulling it out while rinsing the shrimp under cold running water. Repeat with the rest of the shrimp.
- Place the shrimp and marinade in a medium-size glass bowl, mix well, and refrigerate for 10 to 15 minutes.
- Wash the Chinese parsley, dry it with a paper towel, and chop it into small pieces. Measure 2 tablespoons.

Get set . . .

- Wash the red pepper and cut in half. Remove the stem and seeds and discard. Cut the pepper into slices and then into 1/2-inch pieces.

- Slice the green onion into 1/4-inch pieces.
- Line up these ingredients on your countertop: peanut oil, shrimp, red pepper, green onion, Chinese parsley.

Cook!

- Heat a wok on medium heat for 15 seconds. Add 2 tablespoons of the peanut oil.
- After 30 seconds, add the shrimp a few at a time. Stir-fry for 2 to 3 minutes, or just until the shrimp turn pink. Remove the shrimp to a warm plate.
- Add the remaining 1 tablespoon oil to the wok. After 30 seconds, add the red pepper and stir-fry for 1 minute.
- Add the green onion, Chinese parsley, and shrimp. Stir-fry for about 1 minute, or until all the ingredients are well combined.
- Serve hot with rice.

Beggar's Chicken *Qi Gai Ji*

The legend goes that a very long time ago, this dish was created by a beggar who had stolen a chicken from a farmer. The beggar built a fire and put the chicken on a stick to roast it. Suddenly he heard the thunder of horses' hooves. *The farmer!* He quickly pulled the chicken off the fire, wrapped it in a lotus leaf, and buried it in the mud next to the fire. When the farmer came, he searched for his missing chicken but could not find it anywhere, so he galloped away. After he was gone, the beggar dug up the chicken. What a discovery! The mud around the lotus leaf had baked to a hardened clay. When the beggar cracked it open, he found a perfectly cooked, flavorful, and very moist chicken inside. He was very happy with his creation and ate the entire thing. This recipe for Beggar's Chicken comes from the western region of China.

Serves 6

Ingredients

4 cups self-rising flour
1 1/2 cups milk
3 tablespoons canola oil
extra flour for kneading
6 medium-size boneless skinless chicken
    breasts (preferably organic)

1/2 pound ground pork
1 green onion, chopped
1 stalk celery, chopped
1/4 cup chopped bamboo shoots
1 teaspoon salt
1 tablespoon hoisin sauce

On your mark . . .

- **Place the flour in a large bowl. Combine the milk and 1 tablespoon of the canola oil, pour into the flour, and mix well into a soft dough.**
- **Turn the dough out onto a floured surface and knead until it is smooth. This will take a minute or two.**
- **Wrap the dough in plastic wrap or wax paper, place in a clean bowl, and cover with a kitchen towel. Let the dough rest at room temperature for about 30 to 40 minutes.**
- **Wash the chicken under cold running water and pat dry with paper towels. Place the chicken on a platter, cover, and refrigerate until ready to use. Wash the work area where the chicken was cleaned. Be sure to use lots of hot, soapy water and wipe the surfaces dry.**

Get set . . .

- Heat a wok on medium-high heat for 30 seconds. Add 1 tablespoon of the canola oil and heat for a few more seconds.
- Add the ground pork and cook for 4 to 6 minutes, or until the meat browns slightly. Using a spatula, remove the pork to a clean bowl.

- Reheat the wok and add the remaining 1 tablespoon oil. Add the green onion, celery, and bamboo shoots, and stir-fry for 2 minutes.
- Return the pork to the pan and add the salt and hoisin sauce. Cook for another minute or two, making sure all the ingredients are well combined. This is the stuffing. You will need to let it cool completely in a bowl, cover, and refrigerate until ready to use.

Cook!

- **Preheat the oven to 375°F.**
- Unwrap the dough and cut it into 3 pieces. Then cut each of the pieces in half. Take 1 piece of dough and cover the rest with a clean cloth.

- Lightly flour the work surface. Using a rolling pin, roll out the dough to make a circle about 6 inches wide and 1/8-inch thick.

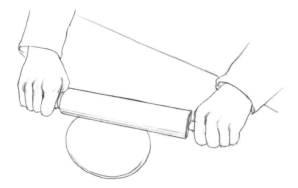

- Lay 1 chicken breast in the center of the dough and top with 1 1/2 tablespoons of the stuffing. Gently fold the dough up over the chicken and stuffing and press together at the edges to seal. Place the chicken in a well-greased baking pan.

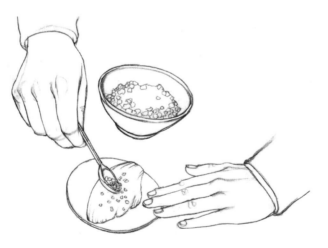

- Repeat these steps with all the dough and chicken breasts.
- Bake for 45 to 50 minutes, basting the chicken with the juices in the bottom of the pan once or twice during the baking.
- Use a spatula to lift the chicken out of the baking pan when it is done.
- Serve hot.

Desserts

Moon Cakes (page 64) and
Almond Cookies (page 62)

Almond Cookies *Xin Ren Bing*

You may recognize these cookies from many Chinese restaurants you may have visited. Though the cookie was not invented in China, the Chinese people have certainly made it a part of their cuisine. This recipe makes a dozen crisp, large cookies. If you have any leftovers, you can freeze them.

Serves 12

Ingredients

2 cups all-purpose flour
1/2 teaspoon baking powder
1/4 teaspoon baking soda
3/4 cup sugar
1 egg

2 tablespoons milk
2 teaspoons almond extract
1/2 cup melted butter (1 stick)
extra flour for kneading
12 whole shelled almonds

On your mark . . .

- Sift together the flour, baking powder, and baking soda into a large bowl. Add the sugar and mix.
- In a small bowl, combine the egg, milk, and almond extract.
- Pour the melted butter into the flour mixture, and then add the milk mixture. Use a fork to combine all the ingredients and form into a soft dough.
- Sprinkle some flour on a very clean countertop or cutting board and on your hands. Turn the dough out onto the countertop.
- Gather the dough together into a ball and gently knead for a few seconds. Shape the dough into a log about 12 inches long. Wrap the cookie dough log in plastic wrap or wax paper and refrigerate for at least 30 minutes.

Get Set . . .

- Place an oven rack in the middle of the oven. **Preheat the oven to 400°F.**
- After the dough has chilled, unwrap it and place it on a lightly floured surface. Cut into 12 sections. Roll each section into a ball.
- Now carefully place 1 ball on a lightly greased baking sheet. Using your thumb, gently make a dent in the center of the ball, flattening it just a little. Place 1 almond in the dent.
- Repeat until all the cookies are formed. Keep them evenly spaced on the baking sheet so they will have room to spread out as they bake.

Cook!

- Bake the cookies for 17 to 20 minutes, or until they are just lightly browned.
- Using a spatula, lift them gently onto a rack and cool completely.

Moon Cakes *Yue Bing*

These special cakes are made in China to celebrate the Moon Festival. The Moon Festival is held at harvesttime, in the eighth month of the Chinese calendar, which is based on the lunar year. The festival generally falls in September on the Western calendar. At festival time, people gather all across China to celebrate and exchange gifts. The most popular gift is a box of four moon cakes. The fillings in the cakes vary from region to region. Here is an adaptation of one classic recipe. You can be creative in choosing the preserves for the filling. What is your favorite?

24 moon cakes

Ingredients

Cake

¾ cup butter (1 ½ sticks)
4 cups all-purpose flour
¾ cup nonfat dry milk
1 teaspoon salt
1 tablespoon baking powder
3 eggs
1 cup sugar
1 teaspoon vanilla extract
extra flour for kneading

Filling

1 cup raspberry preserves (or your choice of
 fruit preserves)
½ cup chopped walnuts
½ cup dried sweetened coconut
½ teaspoon ground cinnamon

24 foil cupcake cups

On your mark . . .

- **Melt the butter over low heat and let it cool.**
- **Combine the flour, nonfat dry milk, salt, and baking powder in a large bowl and mix together.**
- **Sift the flour mixture into a separate large bowl.**
- **In a large mixing bowl, beat the eggs and sugar with an electric hand mixer on low speed for 2 minutes.**
- **Add the cooled butter, vanilla, and flour mixture. Beat on low speed until the ingredients form a sticky dough. This will take about 2 minutes.**
- **Sprinkle some flour on a very clean countertop or cutting board and on your hands. Turn the dough out onto the countertop and knead for about 20 seconds, or until smooth.**
- **Shape the dough into a log 12 inches long and about 2 inches high. Wrap in plastic wrap and refrigerate for at least 30 minutes.**
- **Meanwhile, combine all the ingredients for the filling and set aside. Clean your work area.**

Get Set . . .

- **Preheat the oven to 375°F.** Place 24 foil cupcake cups on 2 baking sheets.
- After the dough has chilled, remove it from the refrigerator and cut it in half. You will have two 6-inch logs. Wrap 1 log and return it to the refrigerator.
- Using a ruler, cut the other log into twelve 1/2-inch slices. Cover the cut slices so they won't dry out.

Cook!

- Take 1 slice of dough and roll it into a ball. Using the palm of your hand, gently flatten the ball into a 4-inch circle.
- Add 1 teaspoon of the filling to the center. Lift the edges of the dough up and over the filling and pinch the edges closed. Gently shape the filled dough to fit a foil cup and place it inside. Don't worry if it doesn't look perfect.
- Repeat until all the slices are filled and shaped. Then cut the other dough log into slices, and fill and shape them.
- Bake the cakes for 25 minutes, or until they are golden brown on top.
- Ask your adult assistant to help you take the cakes out of the oven. Using a spatula, lift them onto a rack to cool completely. Remove the foil cups.
- Moon cakes can be wrapped individually in colored paper, or served on a tray.

HELPFUL KITCHEN EQUIPMENT AND UTENSILS

CHINESE DIPPER

The dipper looks just like a soup ladle, except it is a little wider. It is used to ladle out liquids or to add them while you cook.

CHINESE SPATULA

This is a very handy cooking tool. It looks like the spatulas used in Western kitchens but has a longer handle and a slightly rounded front edge. The edge is shaped to match the wok's rounded form, so it is just right for stir-frying.

CHINESE STRAINER

A strainer is used to lift foods out of liquids. The Chinese strainer has a bamboo handle that will not get hot when you use it.

ELECTRIC RICE COOKER

There are many varieties of electric rice cookers on the market. They all do a good job of making a great batch of rice. If you use an electric cooker, it is recommended that you wash the rice before you cook it to remove the extra starch.

GARLIC PRESS

This amazing little invention is in fact from Italy, not China. A garlic press is perfect not only for pressing garlic but also for pressing fresh ginger.

Tongs are hinged at the top and used like pinchers to pick up or turn over ingredients. Every kitchen needs a good pair of tongs for safely and conveniently handling hot foods.

WOK

The wok is one of the oldest cooking utensils in the world. It dates back thousands of years. The wok is also the most versatile cooker you can use, because it allows you to stir-fry, deep-fry, steam, and even smoke ingredients. Most importantly, it concentrates the heat in just the right way so that foods cook quickly. Most woks today are made out of rolled carbon steel, light iron, or stainless steel. There are also electric woks with nonstick surfaces, but they are not as popular, and they can never get as hot as the traditional wok.

The Chinese wok is shaped like a large bowl, with high sides, either a flat or a round bottom, and a long wooden handle.

If you have an electric stove, you should use a flat-bottom wok, because it will stand on the burner better. By adding a wok ring, you can use a round-bottom wok on an electric stove. The best way to use a wok on an electric stove is to keep one burner—preferably the one next to the burner you are using—free of pots. That way, if the heat gets too high, you can move the wok to the empty, cold burner.

When shopping for a wok, look for one that is fourteen inches in diameter. Follow the manufacturer's instructions for seasoning the cooking surface, and your wok will last for years of perfect meals.

WOK COVER

The cover for a wok is generally made out of aluminum and has a handle on top. Covering the wok makes it the perfect utensil for steaming or boiling.

WOK RING

The wok ring keeps the wok from moving or sliding while you cook. If you have a round-bottom wok, don't use it without the ring.

ESSENTIAL INGREDIENTS IN THE CHINESE KITCHEN

BAMBOO SHOOTS

Bamboo shoots are just what the name says they are: the young edible shoots of the bamboo tree. They are harvested as soon as they make their first appearance above the ground. Bamboo shoots are available canned. Once you open the can, rinse the shoots under cold running water to remove any bitter flavor. They are already cooked, so they are perfect for fast-cooking stir-fried dishes. Once opened, they will keep for about two weeks in a closed container of fresh water. The water should be changed two or three times a week to ensure freshness.

BEAN SPROUTS

Bean sprouts have been a part of Chinese cuisine for more than three thousand years. They are very nutritious and fun to eat. There are two varieties of bean sprouts. The mung bean sprout is white in color, chubby, and very crunchy. The soybean sprout is longer, and it has a tiny soybean at the end. Buy sprouts fresh and keep them in a clean plastic bag. It is a good idea to punch some holes in the bag, so the sprouts will have air. Buy only the amount you need, because sprouts don't keep much longer than three or four days.

BOK CHOY

This green vegetable is sometimes called Chinese cabbage. Bok choy is China's most popular vegetable. It is native to China and its flavor is sweet and mild. When raw, it is very crisp. Look for rich green and white color in the leaves and make sure there are no brown spots. This vegetable is quite different from cabbage in flavor and texture, but cabbage may be substituted if bok choy is unavailable. Napa cabbage is a good substitute. Both bok choy and napa cabbage will keep their freshness for about a week in the refrigerator.

CHILI PEPPERS

Be very careful when you handle some varieties of chilies, because they can be hot! When you do cook with hot chilies, wear rubber gloves to protect your skin, and be very careful not to touch your eyes or mouth. Chili peppers can be used fresh or dried, and they add great flavor to a dish. The jalapeño pepper is one popular variety, but use it in small amounts. It's hot! Dried and powdered chilies like cayenne pepper are easy to use. Start out with a very small amount until you discover just how hot you want your cooking to taste.

CILANTRO, OR CHINESE PARSLEY

Cilantro is an herb also known as fresh coriander or Chinese parsley. Cilantro looks almost identical to parsley and is easily confused with it, but it has a bolder flavor and a spicy aroma. It should be washed to remove any sand still clinging to the stems or leaves and then dried in paper towels. Wrap it in plastic and it will keep for about a week in the refrigerator.

COOKING OILS

Peanut and sesame oils are very common in Chinese cooking, and they add a lot of flavor to many dishes. Peanut oil is used for stir-frying and deep-frying because it has a high smoking point, which means that it can cook at high temperatures before it begins to smoke. Sesame oil, which is made from sesame seeds that have been toasted and pressed, is more delicate and is added to dishes for its rich flavor. It smokes very quickly, however, and is not recommended for high temperatures. The Chinese cook often pours a small amount of sesame oil on steamed fish before serving to add delicious flavor. Another good oil to use for frying is canola. Canola oil is lighter in flavor than peanut oil and a little lower in saturated fat and calories.

EGG ROLL WRAPPERS

Egg roll wrappers can be bought in the supermarket. Once you open the package, use the amount you need and freeze the rest. As you work with the wrappers, make sure to keep them covered, or they will dry out. If they are frozen, thaw them fully before using. You can substitute spring roll wrappers for egg roll wrappers. Spring roll wrappers are not made with eggs, so they are thinner and a little harder to work with.

GINGER OR GINGER ROOT

Ginger is a very important spice in Chinese cooking. When you shop for fresh ginger, look for a nice smooth skin and no dark spots. Peel off the outer skin with a potato peeler. Then slice off the amount the recipe calls for, using a sharp knife. Tightly wrap the remaining piece in plastic wrap and refrigerate. Ginger will keep in the refrigerator for up to two weeks. It can also be frozen. You can use a garlic press to crush ginger. A grater also works to get the juice out of it. Ginger is spicy and too much can make a dish hot, so be careful when you use it.

HOISIN SAUCE

This thick, sweet sauce is made from soybeans, spices, mild chilies, and sugar. Be careful not to confuse it with plum sauce or fish sauce, which have quite different flavors. Once you open the jar, refrigerate it. It will keep for up to six months.

OYSTER SAUCE

Made from oysters and spices, oyster sauce has had a place in the Chinese kitchen for hundreds of years. Once you open the bottle, keep it refrigerated and it will stay fresh for up to six months.

SESAME SEEDS

These tiny, nutty, very flavorful seeds have been used in Chinese cooking for centuries. Sesame seeds may be black, white, yellow, or brown, and they are often toasted for added flavor.

SHIITAKE MUSHROOMS

These mushrooms come fresh or dried. You must soak the dried mushrooms in warm or hot water for at least thirty minutes to revive them. Dried shiitake mushrooms give your recipes a deep, smoky flavor. They will keep for a very long time in an airtight container. A glass jar with a lid works well for storing dried mushrooms.

SOYBEANS

The Chinese have cooked with soybeans for thousands of years. These small beans are real giants of the food world. You could say the soybean is the King of Nutrition. One pound of soybeans has more protein than one pound of steak. In fact, soybeans contain more protein than any other plant in the world! The soybean is also the main source of the world's cooking oil. The list of products made from this little bean is very impressive. Tofu, soy sauce, soy milk, and soybean sprouts are just a few of the foods that come from the soybean.

SOY SAUCE

For three thousand years, soy sauce has flavored the foods of China. There are two main types of soy sauce, light and dark. Both are rich and delicious. Soy sauce has many uses, but be careful—too much can overpower the flavor of a dish. An opened bottle of sauce will keep at room temperature for six to nine months.

TOFU

Made from soybeans, tofu is a wonderful source of protein. By itself, plain tofu has very little flavor, but it has the ability to absorb the flavors of the other ingredients in a dish. It can pick up all the delicious tastes in a stir-fried dish or a hot and sour soup. Tofu is also available in a variety of new flavors and textures. It is sold in soft, medium, firm, or extra firm cakes. For the recipes in this book, use firm or extra firm. Tofu comes packed in water and must be kept refrigerated. When you get it home, remove it from the container and rinse it. Place it in a jar, add fresh water, cover, and refrigerate. Change the water every day to keep the tofu from turning sour. Use it within a week.

INDEX

METRIC CONVERSION CHART

You can use the chart below to convert from U.S. measurements to the metric system.

Weight
1 ounce = 28 grams
1/2 pound (8 ounces) = 227 grams
1 pound = .45 kilograms
2.2 pounds = 1 kilogram

Liquid volume
1 teaspoon = 5 milliliters
1 tablespoon = 15 milliliters
1 fluid ounce = 30 milliliters
1 cup = 240 milliliters (.24 liters)
1 pint = 480 milliliters (.48 liters)
1 quart = .95 liter

Length
1/4 inch = .6 centimeter
1/2 inch = 1.25 centimeters
1 inch = 2.5 centimeters

Temperature
100°F = 40°C
110°F = 45°C
212°F = 100°C (boiling point of water)
350°F = 180°C
375°F = 190°C
400°F = 200°C
425°F = 220°C
450°F = 235°C
(To convert temperatures in Fahrenheit to Celsius, subtract 32 and multiply by .56)